5-15-11

Mackenzie —

You are a sp[...]
to us. We love everything
about you... and hope your
1st communion is a day
you will always remember.
Praying the rosary will
always keep you close to
God.

Love. ♡ Mimi, Mike, Matt, MK,
Joe & Tubs.

Child's Guide to the Rosary

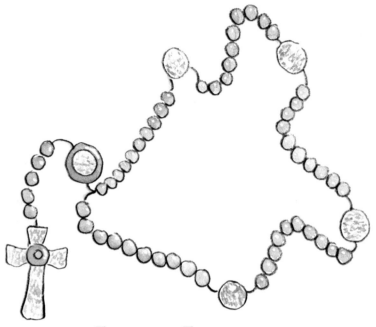

Elizabeth Ficocelli

Illustrations by Anne Catharine Blake

Paulist Press
New York/Mahwah, N.J.

For Tricia Wessels,
whose love for the Rosary and all things Catholic
is a true inspiration
E.F.

For my wonderful stepdaughter,
Elizabeth Hoynes DuFour
A.C.B.

To retain the familiar language of prayers and rites, Scripture quotations are from several sources: the Douay-Rheims Version of the Bible. Also, both the Revised and the New Revised Standard Versions of the Bible, copyright © 1952, 1971, 1989 by the Division of Christian Education of the National Council of Churches of Christ in the U.S.A. Used by permission.

Caseside design by Sharyn Banks
Caseside illustration by Anne Catharine Blake
Book design by Lynn Else

Library of Congress Cataloging-in-Publication

Ficocelli, Elizabeth.
    Child's guide to the Rosary / Elizabeth Ficocelli ; illustrations by Anne Catharine Blake.
      p. cm.
    ISBN 978-0-8091-6736-4 (alk. paper)
    1. Rosary—Juvenile literature. I. Blake, Anne Catharine. II. Title.
    BX2163.F47 2009
    242´.74—dc22
                                                                    2008039588

Published by Paulist Press
997 Macarthur Boulevard
Mahwah, New Jersey 07430

www.paulistpress.com

Printed and bound in Mexico

Hi! My name is Vincent. Today our class is going to talk about the *Rosary*. The Rosary is a special prayer that has been said for many years on beads like these. It tells the story of Jesus and his mother Mary.

Our teacher asked each of us to present a part of this story, or a *Mystery*. We call them Mysteries because each one gives us a lot to think about and no one can understand them completely. There are **Joyful Mysteries**, **Luminous Mysteries**, **Sorrowful Mysteries**, and **Glorious Mysteries**. The students at table one are going to start by talking about the five Joyful Mysteries. These are happy stories about the birth of Jesus and the time when he was a little boy.

The First Joyful Mystery is the Annunciation. The angel Gabriel tells Mary she is going to have a baby. *"Hail, full of grace,"* the angel greets her. *"The Lord is with you! Do not be afraid, Mary, for you have found favor with God. And behold, you will conceive in your womb and bear a son, and you shall call his name Jesus"* (Luke 1:26–31). What surprising and happy news!

I'm glad that Mary said *yes* to God's plan. Mary, help me to say *yes* to God, too.

The Second Joyful Mystery is the Visitation. Mary visits her cousin Elizabeth, who is also going to have a baby. Before Mary can tell her cousin the good news about the baby growing in her tummy, Elizabeth cries out joyfully, *"Blessed are you among women, and blessed is the fruit of your womb!"* (Luke 1:39–42).

Is there someone who might enjoy a visit from me?

The Third Joyful Mystery is the Nativity, the Birth of Baby Jesus. Mary wraps her newborn son in a little blanket and lays him in a manger, because there is no room for them at the inn. The shepherds are in the field that night. An angel appears to them and says, *"Be not afraid; for behold, I bring you good news of a great joy which will come to all the people; for to you is born this day in the city of David a Savior, who is Christ the Lord"* (Luke 2:10–11).

Mary, Joseph, and the shepherds all adored Baby Jesus. Mary, teach me to adore Jesus, too.

The Fourth Joyful Mystery is the Presentation. Mary and Joseph bring Baby Jesus to the Temple to present him to the Lord. An old man named Simeon is in the Temple. He has waited all his life for a savior to be born for his people, and when he sees Baby Jesus, he is full of joy. He praises God, saying, *"My eyes have seen your salvation"* (Luke 2:30). Simeon also knows that Jesus and his mother will suffer, and he tells this to Mary. Mary is sad to hear this news, but she trusts God.

How do *I* feel when I hear upsetting news?

The Fifth Joyful Mystery is the Finding in the Temple. When Jesus is about twelve years old, he gets separated from his parents for three days in the big city of Jerusalem. Mary and Joseph search everywhere. Finally, they find him in the Temple. People are sitting all around him, listening to him talk about God. *"And all who heard him were amazed at his understanding and his answers"* (Luke 2:47).

Mary and Joseph were joyful to have found their son. Mary, help me to stay close to Jesus always.

Table two is going to talk about the five Luminous Mysteries. The word *luminous* means "full of light." These are new mysteries that were added to the Rosary by Pope John Paul II. They tell about important things that Jesus did as a grown-up, when he began to teach people about the kingdom of God.

The First Luminous Mystery is the Baptism of Jesus in the Jordan. Jesus is baptized in the Jordan River by his cousin John the Baptist. As soon as Jesus is baptized, a voice from heaven says, *"This is my beloved Son, with whom I am well pleased"* (Matthew 3:13–17). Now Jesus is ready to go out to teach the people and bring them his Father's love.

Have I been baptized? What does that mean to me?

The Second Luminous Mystery is the Wedding Feast at Cana. Jesus and Mary are at a wedding. There is no more wine for the guests, and Mary lets Jesus know. Then she says to the servants, *"Do whatever he tells you"* (John 2:5). Jesus tells the servants to fill up six large stone jars with water. To their amazement, the water turns to wine! It is Jesus' first public miracle.

Mary, you encourage people to obey your son Jesus. Help me to do as I am told.

The Third Luminous Mystery is the Announcement of the Kingdom. Jesus tells the people, *"The time is fulfilled, and the kingdom of God is at hand; repent, and believe in the gospel"* (Mark 1:14). People travel great distances to hear Jesus talk about love and forgiveness. They come to be healed from their illnesses and forgiven for their sins.

How do I feel when I am forgiven?

The Fourth Luminous Mystery is the Transfiguration. Jesus takes some of the apostles with him to the top of a mountain to pray. As he prays, his face and clothing become dazzling white. Two men from heaven, Moses and Elijah, appear and begin talking to Jesus. As they are talking, a cloud comes over them and a voice from the cloud says, *"This is my Son, my Chosen; listen to him!"* (Luke 9:34–35).

Mary, no one listens better to your son than you. Teach me to listen to him, too.

The Fifth Luminous Mystery is the Institution of the Eucharist. Jesus knows he is going to suffer and die, and that his friends will feel lost without him. So he does something wonderful. He offers his Body and Blood in a special and mysterious way—in a hidden form under the signs of bread and wine. This way, he can be truly present to all of us, every day, in Holy Communion! *And behold, I am with you, until the end of the age"* (Matthew 28:20).

Mary, help me always remember it is Jesus we receive in Holy Communion.

Now, table three is going to talk about the five Sorrowful Mysteries. These are stories of how Jesus suffered and died for us. It makes me sad to think about Jesus suffering, but it is good to remember what he did for us. He loves us so much, he died for us so that one day we can be together in heaven!

The First Sorrowful Mystery is the Agony in the Garden. Jesus is sad and alone. The apostles have fallen asleep. Jesus knows he is going to suffer and it makes him so afraid that he sweats great drops of blood. He prays with all his might. *"And there appeared to him an angel from heaven, strengthening him"* (Luke 22:43).

Do I know someone who is suffering and all alone? What can I do to help them?

The Second Sorrowful Mystery is the Scourging at the Pillar. The soldiers come and take Jesus from the garden. They tie ropes around him and hit him with their fists and insult him with their cruel words. They take him to the governor, Pontius Pilate, who orders the soldiers to whip Jesus for talking about a kingdom and claiming to be a king. *"Then Pilate took Jesus and scourged him"* (John 19:1).

Mary, help me not to hurt others with my words and actions.

The Third Sorrowful Mystery is the Crowning with Thorns. To make fun of Jesus, the soldiers make him a crown out of long, sharp thorns. When they place it on his head, it hurts him and makes him bleed. Next, the soldiers put a red robe on Jesus and pretend to honor him, saying, *"Hail, King of the Jews!"* (Matthew 27:28–29). Jesus is very brave and does not say a word.

Mary, you and I know that Jesus is the true king. Help me to honor him by treating others with respect.

The Fourth Sorrowful Mystery is the Carrying of the Cross. To satisfy the great crowds, the governor tells the soldiers to *crucify* Jesus, or put him to death on a cross. The cross is big and rough and heavy, and the soldiers make Jesus carry it a long way. It is so heavy and Jesus is so weak that he falls down three times. The soldiers take a man from the crowd named Simon and make him help Jesus. *"And they brought Jesus to the place called Golgotha, which means the place of a skull"* (Mark 15:22).

Who needs my helping hand today?

The Fifth Sorrowful Mystery is the Crucifixion. Mary and the apostle John stand at the foot of the cross and watch Jesus suffer. They are very, very sad. Jesus looks at his mother and says, *"Woman, behold your son!"* Then he tells John, *"Behold, your mother!"* (John 19:25–27). From now on, John will take care of Mary. Soon after, Jesus puts his head down and dies.

Mary, your son gave you to all of us, to be our heavenly mother. Watch over me in all I do.

Even though I am sad to think about Jesus dying on the cross, I am happy to remember that three days later, he rose again, just like he said he would! My table, table four, is going to talk about what happened after Jesus died. These are called the five Glorious Mysteries.

The First Glorious Mystery is the Resurrection. After Jesus is taken down from the cross, his body is wrapped in a white cloth and placed in a small cave. A large stone is rolled in front of the opening. On the third day, friends of Jesus discover that the stone has been rolled away. But where is Jesus? Suddenly, an angel appears, saying, *"Do not be afraid. He is not here; for he has risen, as he said"* (Matthew 28:5–6).

Mary, Jesus rose just as he promised he would. Help me to keep my promises, too.

The Second Glorious Mystery is the Ascension. Without Jesus, the apostles are frightened and confused. How overjoyed they are when he appears to them! Jesus stays with his friends for forty days, teaching them and strengthening them. He tells them, *"Go into all the world and preach the gospel to the whole creation"* (Mark 16:15). Then it is time for him to return to the Father. Blessing the apostles one more time, Jesus is lifted from their sight in a cloud of glory.

Who do I know that has died? What will it be like to see that person again in heaven?

The Third Glorious Mystery is the Descent of the Holy Spirit. After Jesus returns to heaven, Mary and the apostles are gathered in a room, praying. Suddenly, a sound like a mighty wind fills the whole house. Something like a flame of fire appears and rests on each one of them, *"and they were all filled with the Holy Spirit"* (Acts 2:4). The apostles then go out, preaching in many languages and healing the sick.

Mary, the Holy Spirit made the apostles excited to tell everyone about Jesus. Help me to be excited, too!

The Fourth Glorious Mystery is the Assumption of Mary. Mary was created free from sin so she can fulfill God's special plan—to carry Baby Jesus in her body. Jesus grows up loving and honoring his mother on earth. So it pleases him to bring his mother up to heaven at the end of her life, complete with her body, *"where she has a place prepared by God"* (Revelation 12:6).

Mary, you suffered with Jesus. Now you are glorified with him. Please pray for all your children on earth.

I have the Fifth Glorious Mystery, which is the Coronation of Mary, Queen of Heaven and Earth. In the Bible, there are many kings, and each one has a queen. But did you know that the queen is usually the king's mother? We know that Jesus is the greatest king of all. That makes his mother Mary the greatest queen. She is *"a woman clothed with the sun, with the moon under her feet, and on her head a crown of twelve stars"* (Revelation 12:1).

Mary, you deserve the crown you wear in heaven. I know you are happy there with your son Jesus. Help us get to heaven, too.

And that's what the Rosary is all about. It's the story of Jesus, just like how the Bible tells it. The Rosary helps us think about and *pray* these stories with the one who knows and loves him best—his mother Mary.

When we pray the Rosary, it helps us to know and love Jesus better.

Do you have your own set of rosary beads? If you don't yet, ask to borrow a set. Then get your rosary beads and join me now.

How to Pray the Rosary

1. Make the **Sign of the Cross** and pray the **Apostles' Creed**.

2. Pray the **Our Father**.

3. Pray **three Hail Marys**.

4. Pray the **Glory Be**.

5. Announce the **Mystery** for reflection and pray the **Our Father**.

6. Pray **ten Hail Marys** (called a "decade").

7. Finish the decade with the **Glory Be**.

Repeat numbers 5, 6, and 7 for each decade.

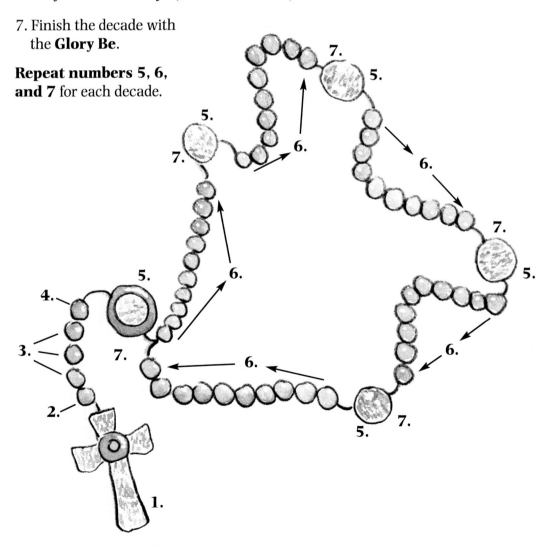

Rosary Prayers

The Sign of the Cross
In the name of the Father, and of the Son, and of the Holy Spirit.
Amen.

The Apostles' Creed
I believe in God the Father Almighty, Creator of heaven and earth;
and in Jesus Christ, his only Son, our Lord;
Who was conceived by the Holy Spirit, born of the Virgin Mary,
suffered under Pontius Pilate, was crucified, died, and was buried.
He descended into hell; the third day he arose again from the dead;
He ascended into heaven, and is seated at the right hand of God,
the Father Almighty;
from there he shall come to judge the living and the dead.
I believe in the Holy Spirit, the Holy Catholic Church, the Communion of Saints,
the forgiveness of sins, the resurrection of the body, and life everlasting.
Amen.

The Our Father
Our Father, who art in heaven, hallowed be Thy name:
Thy kingdom come: Thy will be done on earth as it is in heaven.
Give us this day our daily bread, and forgive us our trespasses
as we forgive those who trespass against us.
And lead us not into temptation: but deliver us from evil.
Amen.

The Hail Mary
Hail Mary, full of grace; the Lord is with thee:
blessed art thou among women, and blessed is the fruit of thy womb, Jesus.
Holy Mary, Mother of God, pray for us sinners,
now and at the hour of our death.
Amen.

The Glory Be
Glory be to the Father and to the Son and to the Holy Spirit,
as it was in the beginning, is now, and ever shall be, world without end.
Amen.

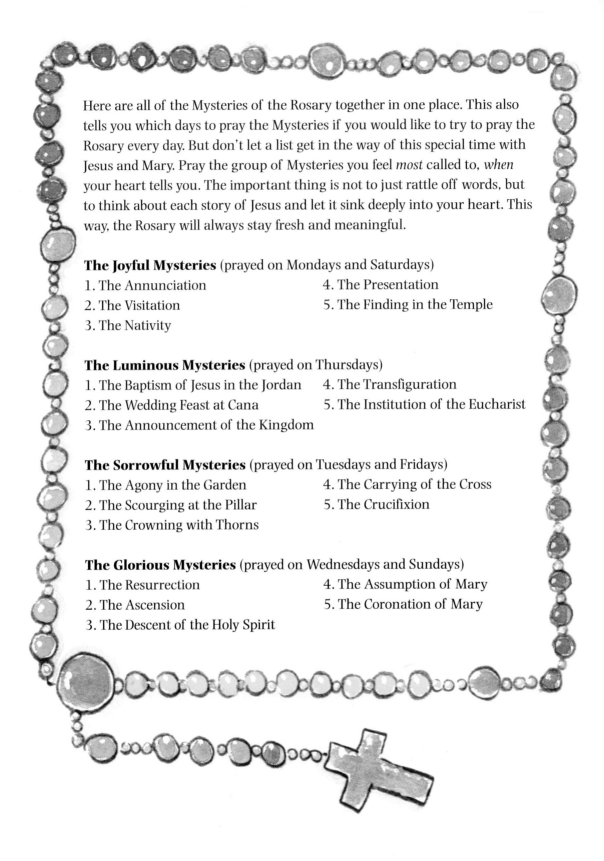

Here are all of the Mysteries of the Rosary together in one place. This also tells you which days to pray the Mysteries if you would like to try to pray the Rosary every day. But don't let a list get in the way of this special time with Jesus and Mary. Pray the group of Mysteries you feel *most* called to, *when* your heart tells you. The important thing is not to just rattle off words, but to think about each story of Jesus and let it sink deeply into your heart. This way, the Rosary will always stay fresh and meaningful.

The Joyful Mysteries (prayed on Mondays and Saturdays)
1. The Annunciation
2. The Visitation
3. The Nativity
4. The Presentation
5. The Finding in the Temple

The Luminous Mysteries (prayed on Thursdays)
1. The Baptism of Jesus in the Jordan
2. The Wedding Feast at Cana
3. The Announcement of the Kingdom
4. The Transfiguration
5. The Institution of the Eucharist

The Sorrowful Mysteries (prayed on Tuesdays and Fridays)
1. The Agony in the Garden
2. The Scourging at the Pillar
3. The Crowning with Thorns
4. The Carrying of the Cross
5. The Crucifixion

The Glorious Mysteries (prayed on Wednesdays and Sundays)
1. The Resurrection
2. The Ascension
3. The Descent of the Holy Spirit
4. The Assumption of Mary
5. The Coronation of Mary